AF582327

U-176
PROJECT REPORT:
Search and Location of a World War II Submarine.

Maximino Gómez Álvarez
Alexander Mirabal Reyes

Translated by: Osvaldo L. Cangas

English Edition

Library of Congress Control Number: 2022912749

ISBN: 9798348117702
Imprint: U-176 Museum-Institute for War Studies Inc..
Miami, FL. 33157
by the
Publishing Departments of AIDHNC & U-176.COM

Asociación para la Investigación y
Difusión de la Historia Naval de Cuba.
&
U-176 Museum-Institute for War Studies Inc.

For reproduction permits and for purchase of this book in quantities for promotional or premium use, discounts and terms,
please contact us at social@u-176.com – www.u-176.com
Mailing Address: 11241 SW 157th Street. Miami, FL. 33157.

DEDICATION

To the "Asociación para la Investigación y Difusión de la Historia Naval de Cuba", who has always encouraged and supported this research and trusted us to carry it out.

CONTENTS

ACKNOWLEDGMENTS

This investigation has been possible thanks to the research of different libraries and archives, therefore, we want to thank all the information provided by the Archives of the AIDHNC; the Uboot Archiv (Cuxhaven) Germany; the files shared by the National Oceanic and Atmospheric Administration NOAA, because without their charts this work would have been very difficult, or rather impossible.

TO ALL, OUR MOST SINCERE RECOGNITION.

- 1 -
SUMMARY

On May 15th, 1943, the German submarine U-176 was sunk in waters near the Island of Cuba, as a result of the action of the CS-13 submarine chaser of the Navy of that Caribbean country and with the assistance of a US aircraft belonging to the VS-62 Squadron based in Cayo Frances, Cuba.

Although it is true that at first the authorities were cautious about proclaiming the success of the action, subsequently and once the conflict was over and the Archives of the Unterseebootsflottille were occupied by the Allies, it was finally possible to prove its sinking.

Today, after more than 70 years have elapsed and considering the historical relevance of what happened and subjecting it to a rigorous study and investigation, in order to establish the coordinates of the resting area of said wreck, with the purpose of being able to carry out the search, location, study and filming "in situ".

For the present work, documents and different primary sources have been consulted, among others, those existing at the National Archives and Records Administration (NARA) and Uboot Archiv; detecting, however, the existence of what we have considered to call "zones of documentary silence" or what is the same, lack of clarifying documents of certain moments of the events described.

Likewise, few secondary sources have been consulted, observing a significant absence of bibliography that addresses this object of study, therefore we turn to the "oral" sources with the aim of covering some of these gaps, which due to their characteristics and complexity, all were subjected to criticism and comparison.

For the study corresponding to the technical analysis of the location, the NOAA charts were studied, with the bathymetry (data of the marine currents in the search perimeter) corresponding to the month of May 1943, the date on which the events occurred.

- 2 -
INTRODUCTION

From the very beginning of the Second World War, the fundamental objective of the German submarine fleet was aimed at the systematic sinking of freighters that could carry vital supplies, which would allow the allied countries to successfully confront Nazi Germany.

This concept of Total Submarine Warfare, designed and developed by the German high command with the aim of causing economic suffocation, fundamentally of Great Britain, had its most significant concretion and expression in the Battle of the Atlantic.

The attack on the American base at Pearl Harbor by the naval and air forces of the Japanese Empire on December 7, 1941, precipitated the entry of the United States into the conflict, and with the beginning of hostilities between these two nations, the submarine war entered a new phase, when the Fuhrer Adolf Hitler ordered the lifting of the restrictions in the Pan-American exclusion zone, turning the waters of America into a new theater of war with the so-called Operation Paukenschlag (Operation Drumbeat); days later, the sector of confrontation was extended to the Caribbean and Gulf of Mexico, with the well-known Operation Neuland (Operation New Land), which from that moment until well into 1943, became the main area of confrontation.

The presence and activity of the German u-boats in the Caribbean Sea and the Gulf of Mexico increased more and more and the successes obtained by them created enormous concern in the British; the losses began to be enormous, most of the merchants never reached their destination ports. Prime Minister Winston Churchill himself in a cable sent on March 12th, 1942, to Franklin D. Roosevelt, President of the United States of America stated: "I am most deeply concerned at the immense sinking of tankers west of the 40th meridian and in the Caribbean Sea....The situation is so serious that drastic action of some kind is necessary".

The young Republic of Cuba, due to its strategic position, became one of the main allies of North America. On December 9, 1941, it declared war against the Japanese Empire and two days later, on December 11 of the same month, it extended said declaration of war against Italy and Germany in terms similar to that carried out against Japan, thus placing country at the head of the Latin-American nations in the confrontation with the Axis forces.

The small Navy of this Caribbean nation had to play an important role in confronting the submarines that roamed its coasts and to carry out this commitment, it signed several naval and air agreements aimed at strengthening its navy and aviation. One of these agreements reached allowed the transfer to Cuba of a total of 12 (twelve) 83-foot submarine chaser units, as part of the Lend-Lease Act, as well as the training of their crews (Cubans) sent to US territory, which strengthened substantially its anti-submarine capability.

As a result of the participation of the Navy of the Republic of Cuba (Marina de Guerra de Cuba) in this conflict, the German submarine U-176 sank, which since then rests in Cuban territorial waters, without any known attempt having been made to search for and locate it.

With this project, whose main objectives from the technical and archaeological point of view are, first, the resting place of the remains of the submarine on the seabed using side-scan sonar technology and, second, to explore and document videographic and photographic the body of the wreck through underwater robotic technology operated remotely from the surface, seeks to answer various questions, both historical and environmental, and even human, which, without the necessary technological capacity to achieve direct visual contact with the wreck, have remained in the realm of the unknown for over seventy years:

- Where exactly are the remains of U-176: How far from the "official" sinking site? How big was the fault that caused the damage? Did this occur at one end of the boat -bow or stern-, where the rooms of torpedoes were located, corroborating the hypothesis of an internal explosion?

- How could the existing marine currents influence the area where the sinking of the submarine took place, in its trajectory of descent to reach the sea floor?

-What influence could the damage caused by the attack exert on the structure of the submarine, and in its line of descent until the final resting point?

The correlation of the answers to these questions, in addition to the knowledge that they themselves contain could, for example, shed light on issues such as the cautious reaction of U.S. Naval authorities regarding the outcome of the incident, attributed by some Cuban scholars, to the interest of those authorities to snatch that victory from the Cuban Navy. Or also, to support or at once refute "legends" that have reached space within serious documents, one of them authored by Norberto Collado (CS-13 sonar operator), where he refers to a Chilean diver who during a competition of "underwater fishing", managed to see the wreck in its resting place.

- Are the submarine's fuel tanks still physically intact, or the area of batteries that fed the electrical propulsion system? if so the case, with the inevitable collapse of the structure due to time and the action of the sea on the metal, it is to be assumed that said contents will be released to the outside. If, on the other hand, they have already been released, is there any type of visible impact -from the environmental point of view- in the area due to this?

- Would it be possible - in the opinion of experts in the field, and based on the images obtained - that human remains are still preserved inside the wreck? It is a question and a situation of great sensitivity, since there are still living descendants of some sailors who perished in the submarine.

The lack of factual information and prior technical studies of this sinking caused the need to start from "zero" and with the scant information available on the "location of the target" (latitude and longitude) at the time of its sinking, an analysis work was developed using different variables, currents, possible angles of inclination in the descent, etc., which led to the hypothesis of establishing 4 Search Zones (ZB), delimited from each other in importance according to the calculations made.

The choice of the search and location of the remains of U-176 as a research topic, apart from its technical scientific interest, has been chosen, in addition, for its historical relevance that makes it a focus of attention due to the significance it holds for the group of nations that were involved in the conflict (submarine warfare), especially for the United States, Germany and Cuba.

What reasons can be put forward to justify the search and location of U-176?

a-) The presence of the submarine was detected by a reconnaissance aircraft from the United States.

b-) The Submarine Chaser boat (CS-13) that sank it had been transferred by the United States to Cuba through the Lend Lease Act.

c-) It is the only u-boat sunk by a Latin American Navy, which constitutes a milestone in the Naval History of that continent, recognized by Admiral and Historian Samuel Elliot Morison in his work "The Two-Ocean War: A Short History of the United States Navy in the Second World War" Pg. # 119.

d-) The Cuban crew received training in the United States, especially their sonar operators (Subchaser Training Center of Miami, Florida), who despite their inexperience, put out of action to one of the most powerful submarine vessels of the time, a Type IXC (long range) U-boat, which had an efficient and experienced crew and commander, not because the textbooks indicate it, but because such an affirmation was personally provided by Alfred Eick, 1st. Officer of said submarine (he survived because he did not participated in the last patrol of this u-boat), in an interview we held with him in the city of Bieliefeeld.

The U-176 had already survived the furious attack of HMS Viscount and later escaped 3 depth charges dropped by a Catalina aircraft, all due to the expertise of its captain, who was considered an extremely capable leader, disciplined and sometimes stubborn, and the latter is proven by history itself; the U-176 chased the freighter "Polydorus" for approximately 55 hours until it was sunk, considered the longest chase carried out by a submarine to sink its prey.

The Commander of U-176, Korvettenkapitän Reiner Dierksen, for his ability, dedication and bravery was decorated with:

1940	Iron Cross 2nd Class.
1940	Minesweeper War Badge.
3 Oct 1942	Iron Cross 1st Class.
19 Feb 1943	U-boat War Badge 1939.
7 Jan 1944	German Cross in Gold (posthumous).

e-) The day before its sinking, this submarine had torpedoed and sunk an American vessel, the "SS Nickeliner" and another Cuban vessel, the "SS Mambí".

f-) If, for example, we consider the enormous media repercussion, both in the United States and in the rest of the world (television, cinema, press, etc.) that the discovery of the U-166 had seventy kilometers from the Mississippi delta,which had been sunk in 1942 by depth charges launched by the escort ship USS PC-566, we find that Hans-Gunter Kuhlmann was an inexperienced Commander who was never decorated and had a record of only 4 sinkings with a total of 7,593 tons sunk, compared to Reiner Dierksen with 11 sinkings in just 3 patrols and with a total of 53,307 tons sunk, around 7.02 times more than the tonnage achieved by the U-166.

U-176 going out from port to one of its three patrols.

Members of the VS-62 Squadron, behind them is the Vought Sikorsky Kingfisher which detected the presence of U-176 on May 15th, 1943.

- 3 -
BACKGROUND

During the information gathering process, the scarce bibliographical information, articles and primary sources where everything related to the sinking of the U-176 has been studied or narrated were consulted, observing the absence of previous studies of any other author who addresses the attempt to locate and search for this wreck, therefore focusing on the consultation of primary sources located in different Archives and trying through oral sources, through "unstructured interviews", to collect as much information as possible. It would allow us to recompose what happened historically, while providing us with information that could be used in the technical analysis of the sinking.

This lack of sources and limited volume of information, although it was an obstacle, did not significantly affected the conclusions reached in the result of the investigation.

- 4 -
FACTS ABOUT THE INCIDENT.

At 11:00 p.m. on May 12, 1943, the Cuban-flagged ship "Mambí" of the Cuban Distilling Company, loaded with honey, and the American-flagged tanker "Nickeliner", which was transporting ammonia, set sail from the Port of Nuevitas, both escorted by two submarine chasers of the Cuban Navy, forming Convoy NC-18. At 04:00 hours on May 13, and 6 miles from Faro Manatí, both merchant vessels were unexpectedly torpedoed by a u-boat, which, after carrying out its successful attack, made a rapid dive, while undertaking a stealthy and rapid evasion action, with which he managed to escape from the response of the submarine chasers. The two merchant ships sank, and as a result there were considerable losses of human life and material.

Two days after the fatal event, the merchant ships "SS Camagüey" and "SS Wanks" flying Cuban and Honduran flags, respectively, left the Port of Nuevitas, advancing at the speed of 8 knots, the regulation speed for convoys, and flanked by 3 Cuban submarine chasers. One of the escort vessels, the CS-22, was constantly moving, placing itself on one side or the other of the merchant ships in a clear cover maneuver; CS-11, Chief of the Escort, was traveling in the front of the convoy, and CS-13 was closing the protection, thus taking extreme protection knowing that those waters were being prowled by a u-boat.

At 5:15 p.m. at latitude 23°.21N and longitude 80°.18W, appeared a US Navy seaplane, a Vougt Sikorsky Kingfisher, belonging to the VS-62 Squadron based at the North American Naval Air Station in Cayo Francés, Cuba, which was making a routine flight, which when approaching the place, detected the presence of an enemy submarine due to the glare caused by sunlight reflecting on the periscope lens.

The plane immediately went to the place of the sighting and was able to observe the silhouette of the submarine in the water; in this way, while making radio contact with the escort, it began to move its wings and to turn off and on the engine according to the agreed signal, then launching a smoke bomb to mark the location and began to fly describing circles around the drop zone, about a mile and a half to starboard from the stern of the ship that led the escort. The Commander of CS-11 placed his forces on alert in the face of the imminent presence of a submarine, ordering by radio the CS-13, commanded by Ensign (Alférez) Mario Ramírez Delgado, to go to the area indicated by the plane and to engage in combat.

The convoy turned 45° to port and by then the CS-13 was already heading at full speed, at a speed of 15 knots, in the direction of the confrontation zone. Approaching within 360 meters of the target, the CS-13 sonar operator established contact with the enemy submarine, whose sound turned out to be very clear with marked "doppler" effect and propeller noise; the target then moved hastily and began a rapid dive upon being discovered and threatened; It was then that the Commander of the submarine fighter ordered to rotate 25° on the target to carry out the attack, producing the launch of a first depth charge, preset at 30 meters, followed by two others at 46 and 61 meters respectively, changing the course between the second and third charges, to correct for any additional speed applied by the submarine in its attempt to escape.

The first two charges exploded normally and caused the rise of two enormous columns of foamy and clear water, however, after the third explosion a fourth was heard, presumably caused by the explosion of the torpedo room of the submarine, and this time the explosion was of such magnitude that the submarine chaser (CS-13) submerged its bow in the water, which then penetrated to the engine room.
This last explosion, however, was accompanied by a column of muddy brown water that rose much higher than the previous ones, then the submarine fighter turned to port and cut its engines; the sonar device recovered contact with the target at about 122 meters, but this time there was no movement, no engine noise, and no doppler effect; the

contact was very clear and metallic, according to the sonar operator, who then told the captain of the ship that what he had heard could not come from the swirls caused by the depth charges.

The Commander of the boat thought that the submarine was standing still and proceeded to order the engines to be turned off, thus keeping the ship like this for three minutes, after which, he again ordered to start them up and proceed to attack; this time the depth of the U-boat was set at 122 meters, proceeding to a new attack, launching two other depth charges, one at 61 and the other one at 122 meters.

Shortly after the second attack, the CS-13 positioned itself over the area of the last explosion and, again silencing its engines, began a careful acoustic survey; No contact was made then, but something similar to the sound caused by air bubbles in water escaping from a semi-closed container was heard for approximately two minutes, which, in the opinion of Ensign (Alférez) Ramírez and the sonar operator, could not in any case be caused by the launch of the last depth charge, since it had taken place 8 minutes before.

The third charge launched in the first attack produced the appearance of a small fuel slick on the surface of the sea, which increased in size until it reached a diameter of about 270 meters, then the commander of the submarine chaser ordered one of the sailors of the crew to collect, with the help of a bucket and some cloth, samples of that stain to be later analyzed at the Navy Laboratory; unfortunately, said sample was later lost due to heavy seas that then appeared at the height of the coast of Matanzas and the little that could be saved from the sample in the container and on the cloth, in addition to being adulterated, was insufficient for the realization of an accurate chemical analysis. After the attack, the CS-13 remained in the area of the event for two hours, after which it headed at full speed to rejoin the convoy, which occurred around 19:35 hours (7:35 p.m.).

It was difficult to prove the sinking of the submarine, since the evidence that was available in the moments after the narrated events was insufficient and in the case of the oil samples that appeared on the surface, in addition to the fact that no analysis could be carried out , this sample in itself, did not constitute conclusive evidence, since its appearance on the surface could be the result of a "trick" used quite frequently by the Commanders of u-boats, when they were surprised and attacked; that is, they stopped the submarine's engines, maintaining absolute radio silence and ordering the expulsion of oil and garbage through the torpedo tubes, which they kept accumulated in a sealed chamber and whose remains, when reaching the surface, could make the attacking ship believe that it had been successful in the action. This is the reason why the reports, mainly from the file known as Incident 3208, are not categorical when it comes to proving the destruction of this u-boat as certain. However, when the German archives were occupied by the allies, it was clarified that the merchant ships "SS Mambí" and "SS Nickeliner" were sunk by the U176, and that this same submarine was the one that was destroyed by the action of the Cuban submarine chaser, called CS-13.

Cuban Sub-Chaser CS-13 responsible of sinking U-176.

- 5 -
OBJECTIVES OF THIS RESEARCH.

With the available elements, the objective of the investigation was outlined, consisting of locating and determining the coordinates of the resting place of the still existing remains of the German submarine U-176, sunk by the Cuban submarine fighter CS-13 during World War II, through Side Scan Sonar exploration of the proposed area according to the available historical data, as well as its subsequent exploration and documentation through photographic and film records.

U-176 Project Report

- 6 -
GENERAL CONSIDERATIONS REGARDING THE SEARCH.

Succeeding in the search for a wreck, apart from casual factors that at a given moment could play their role for or against, means having an educated idea beforehand of where to look for it.

This begins with the place or area where the sinking of the vessel occurred and is immediately connected with the possible trajectory of the body's fall from the surface to the bottom, and the direction in which it occurred. The fall trajectory of the physical body that constitutes the hull of the vessel is determined, on the one hand, by the thrust force that the sea current exerts on said body in its fall through the different layers of the water depth. At the same time, the magnitude of this effect is something that will depend a lot on the characteristics of the body itself: its size, its shape, the degree of buoyancy it contains. And all this, at the same time, is directly related to the damage caused by its sinking.

In the case of the search for the U-176, it is necessary to manage all these variables, either in a reasonably exact manner, as far as documentary and historical evidence allows us, or by extrapolating experiences and procedures tested in the search for other wrecks that have resulted successful.

U-176 Project Report

- 7 -
GEOGRAPHICAL POSITION. PROBABLE AREA OF SINKING.

The selection of the search area takes as its starting point the geographical reference 23 21 N, 80 18 W, cited in several official reports of the time, as well as in the memoirs of Captain Norberto Collado, whose participation in the action of May 15 of 1943 was protagonist and essential. It is the key data. From it everything else is articulated. However, the accuracy of this baseline geographic datum cited in the reports should be considered conservatively for the following reasons:

- From a technological point of view, the accuracy of the type of instruments used in 1943 for position estimation was far from the standards of current global positioning systems, where sub-metric accuracy is common in relatively inexpensive marine equipment.

- The error contained in said position, moreover, must also be assumed to be significant for reasons of a subjective and operational nature. It is very unlikely that, in the heat of the military action, someone would take care to determine in detail the geographical position in which it was happening, the conditions being very unfavorable in every way to concentrate on a detailed reading of the instruments. It is known, and also cited in some North American naval sources of the time that evaluated the effectiveness of the actions of the different allied navies against German submarines, that the report of the position of sightings and attacks was, as a general rule, very unreliable due to precisely for these reasons. Without being excessively suspicious, the fact that the coordinates handled are "integers" denotes the presence of an approximation behind which lie, numerically, all these factors in the form of an error.

How big could this error be? It is difficult to guess exactly, precisely because of the strong subjective component of its origin, but it is to be assumed that any type of rounding must have been done to the nearest integer value, either by excess or by default.

Assuming that the error in both axes - latitude and longitude - was within +- 2' , then, with respect to the cited position, we would be talking about +- 2 miles.

Thus, everything having happened in the open sea, with no other fixed references on land that could help delimit the place of the action, it is a prudent practice to manage, rather than a sinking site, a Probable Sinking Zone (ZHP) with a radius between 1.5 and 2 miles centered on the position cited in the reports.

7.1- Possible sinkage scenarios and their impact on fall distance.

It is, for many years, an unquestionable fact that the U-176 succumbed to the attack of the SC-13; however, the way in which everything happened -something that for other historical purposes is a matter not so relevant perhaps in light of the final result of the action, but which is vital for the objective of this project- is not entirely clear by as the action took place entirely underwater, without any visual contact from the surface vessels involved.

There are several elements in the available reports, both testimonial and technical, that manage to accommodate some of two fundamental scenarios in terms of the magnitude of the damage caused and the possible evolution of events in depth, sometimes even both scenarios.

This duality of possibilities in terms of scenarios for the evolution of the events possibly explains the certain caution observed in the evaluations of the incident made by the Committee on Assessment of Damage to Enemy Submarines during their meetings in the months following the incident, which ranged from "E" (Probably slightly damaged) to "B" (Probably sunk).

With the same data on the table, it is revealing -but not surprising- the fact that the Committee's evaluation criteria was always cautious (always 'Probably', and initially only 'slightly damaged'), which shows that In effect, they found themselves in an ambiguous situation that did not give them elements to definitively lean towards a more conclusive criterion.

In terms of predicting, in general terms, what the evolution of the body was on its way to the bottom, and therefore, how far it could be from the site of the incident, the extreme scenarios on which we base our analysis are the following:

7.2- Scenario 1: Immediate sinking due to internal explosion.

It is generally the most historically accepted and considers that the third depth charge effectively impacted the submarine - presumably at the bow or stern, where the torpedo rooms were located - and this caused an internal explosion of great magnitude, cited and described in reports as the "fourth explosion".

Fundamental evidence that supports this hypothesis.

- The fourth explosion itself, immediately after the third depth charge launched, and which is widely cited and described in the reports of the time. The explanation that is generally found is that it must have originated internally as a result of the effect of the attacking charge.

- The oil slick that emerged after the fourth explosion, in the place where the depth charge that is assumed to have originated it was dropped, has historically been related to the damage caused to the submarine, not to a deception maneuver.

Foreseeable hydrodynamic implications. Consequences in the sinking trajectory.

Considering the significant demolition effect that torpedoes such as those carried by the U-176 caused on the attacked vessels, and the fact that when leaving its base in Lorient to carry out its 3rd and last patrol, this submarine did so loaded with 18 of these projectiles, of which he had only used two of them during the sinking of the merchant ships "Mambi" and "Nickeliner", therefore carrying 16 of these explosive devices at the time of being attacked, distributed in the stern and bow, it is to be assumed that the internal explosion must have been much more intense than the one caused by the original depth charge, literally demolishing the structure of the vessel, at least in the area of occurrence, thus making it lose its buoyancy capacity and possibly also its propulsion, and finally causing a relatively abrupt descent (to sink), determined by the resulting hydrodynamic characteristics of the affected hull and by the action of the marine currents that this body encountered in its fall along the water depth.

Contradictory data regarding the scenario of a large internal explosion.

- A column of water was produced associated with the fourth explosion, and it was even greater than the previous ones ("...a larger splash than the other charges had given was observed"..). Having been an internal explosion, that is, whose energy release focus was in physical contact with the solid body that represented the boat, and also inside it (which absorbs, at least, an important part of the energy released), the existence of the water column itself, and its mentioned size, are contradictory.

- It is mentioned in a report issued from Havana that, when the CS-13 turned around and reestablished contact with the target after the first attack, it was at a depth of about 122 meters (originally, when the attack began, it had been estimated about 45 - 60 meters). This by itself does not necessarily mean that the increase in depth was not deliberate, since gaining depth was a way of staying "below" the range of the "echo ranging gear" of surface vessels. For others, 122 meters was a depth well below the test (Test depth) mentioned in some sources for these units, which was 230 meters (750 feet). For a commander of Dierksen's character, an extreme evasion maneuver when cornered would not have been unusual.

- The CS-13 finds the target motionless and silent: "no target movement, no engine noises, no Doppler effect". There is no mention of bubbling noise due to water ingress (this is only referred to after the second attack). One might add "no voices, no human noises". This scenario of stillness and silence is more suited to a masking scenario than to one caused by damage such as that caused by a large internal explosion as assumed.

- It is very unlikely that if an explosion of similar magnitude had occurred, the structure would have been left in conditions of relatively neutral buoyancy (being suspended within the water column, "dead in the water" as the report says), as stated by been perceived from the "echo ranging gear" of the CS-13 after reestablishing contact with the target (uboat) and evaluating the situation again, after the first attack.

7.3- Scenario 2: Partial damage, distant sinking.

Here it is assumed that the third charge effectively affected the submarine, but the damage caused (perhaps in propulsion, partially in sealing and ballast control) was not devastating enough to cause an immediate sinking.

Fundamental evidence supporting the hypothesis of partial damage.

- After the first attack, after reestablishing contact with the target to analyze its behavior, the report issued by CS-13 states that the "target" was motionless and silent at 122 meters, and that its width in the "echo ranging gear" was of 5 degrees. From this last datum, when analyzing the necessary conditions for such a measurement result to have been possible, an important conclusion is inferred, which, in fact, was approached in his analysis by a CS-13 officer; Although it is never explicitly mentioned, in its stillness and silence, the submarine was, in addition, significantly inclined towards the bow or stern.

Only if the submarine was longitudinally aligned with respect to the imaginary axis of the acoustic beam emitted by the CS-13 and tilted at an angle approximately similar to that of the CS-13, could such a result have been observed in the sonar image. In this sense, it was truly fortuitous - more useful for the analysis - that in its maneuver, the CS-13 found the target in such conditions. From this it is inferred that the submarine had indeed been damaged; its ability to balance was affected.

The 5 degrees of width of the "target" observed in the "echo ranging gear" of the CS-13, can only be obtained when two particular conditions are met: the submarine is oriented longitudinally on the same axis of the acoustic beam, and that it presents an angle of inclination similar to the aforementioned acoustic beam.

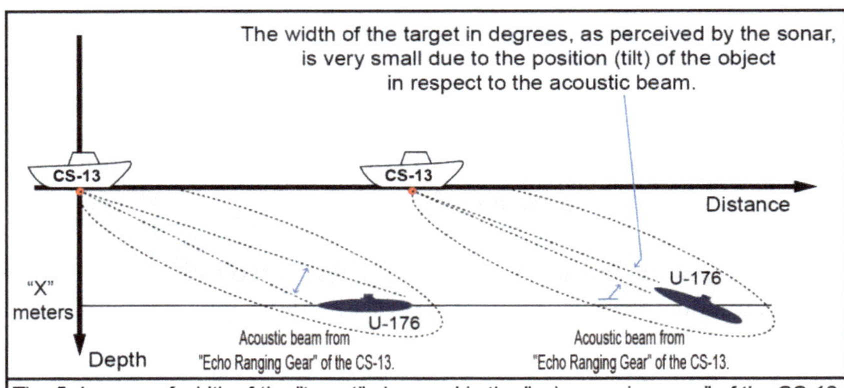

The 5 degrees of width of the "target" observed in the "echo ranging gear" of the CS-13, can only be obtained when two particular conditions are met: the submarine is oriented longitudinally on the same axis of the acoustic beam, and that it presents an angle of inclination similar to the aforementioned acoustic beam.

- With the vessel damaged, and not demolished, a masking maneuver makes sense, such as not turning on machines (if they were in working order), nor generating human noise. Such a situation is what the report cites after the first attack.

- In opposition to the above reasoning, but in accordance with the general idea of this scenario, the mention made by Captain Norberto Collado (CS-13 sonar operator on the day of the events) more than sixty years later in his memoir (strangely not contained in the reports of this event at that time), about clearly hearing on sonar the Commander of the submarine ordering the entire crew to run immediately to the stern - apart from the fact that Collado did not have any knowledge of the German language, nor that it can effectively be taken for granted that the voice he heard was that of Dierksen -, it is also compatible with the conditions described. Whether it was to escape from an area that had lost its watertightness and was flooding, or to try to rearrange the load and give some balance to the damaged submarine, this maneuver would make sense.

Foreseeable hydrodynamic implications. Consequences in the sinking trajectory.

The structure must have retained a certain buoyancy capacity for a time, but having lost ballast control, the inevitable sinking is smooth and slow, -it does not literally go to the bottom quickly-, always at the mercy of the sea current, to a depth in which finally the structure collapses due to pressure, and the sinking then becomes more abrupt.

Contradictory data regarding this scenario.

- The fourth explosion. Its origin, if it had not been internal, is difficult to explain, since said explosion was objectively verified (its effect was heard and seen on the surface), then it would necessarily have originated outside the vessel, and there were only three charges depth launched by the CS-13 during the first attack, there is no apparent source to explain the fourth explosion. There is no historical background to associate such an explosion with some type of deception maneuver practiced by the Germans, or with any torpedo that was launched.

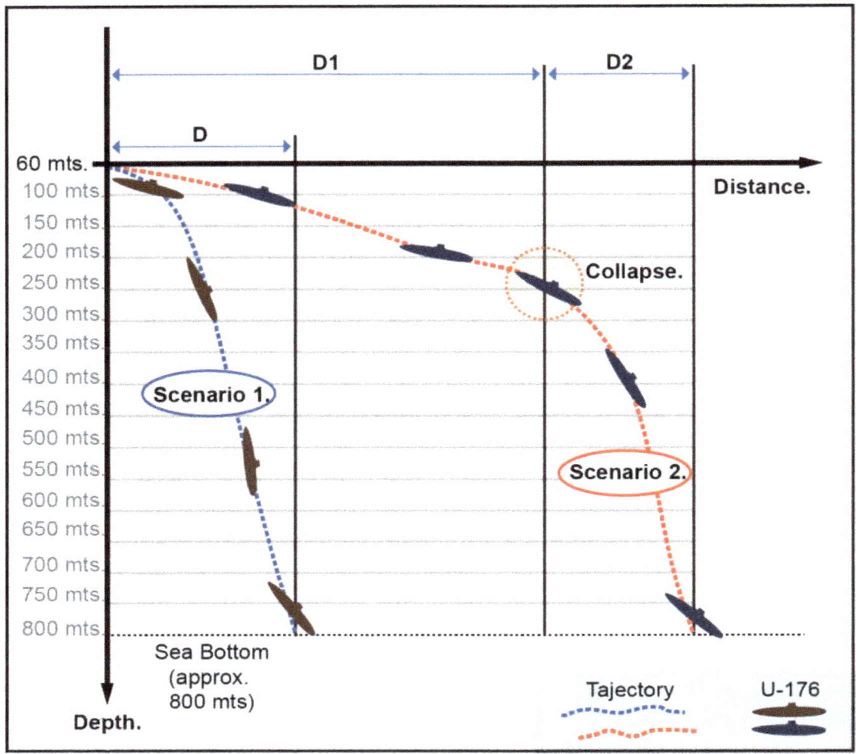

Possible sinking scenarios. 1: Immediate, 2: Delayed.
Note the effect on the distance of the fall in
respect to the point of the incident.

7.4- Criteria adopted to size the Search Zone (ZB).

Although mathematically, from fluid dynamics, the relationship of forces can be described acting on a body and, as a result, its approximate trajectory during its fall, in the case of a shipwreck this exercise is more difficult to practice because it is lacking, practically absolutely, from sufficiently real data about the submerged body: its effective mass -determined by its original characteristics and by the buoyancy that it conserved- and partly on its final form, determined again by its original appearance and by the type of damage that caused its sinking.

As we know that for the purpose of searching for a wreck, a metric precision is not required, but rather an estimate that reasonably includes its probable resting place is often the best practice when it comes to undertake this estimate be based on known antecedents of previous explorations, preferably in areas more or less close, of which the magnitude of the current and the size of the sunken body are known, as well as sinking position, depth and drop point. In this case, we base our estimate on the specific case of the hull of the USS Maine (entirely open and completely flooded), whose horizontal displacement was verified, and was approximately 3 miles during the fall of 1150 meters of depth, pushed by the Gulf Stream off Havana.

In the case of U-176, considering an average depth of 850 meters in the current conditions typical of the Canal de San Nicolas, and following a moderately conservative criterion of buoyancy for the sunken body (so that the second scenario described above is contained to a reasonable degree), it is considered to manage a base extension of approximately 7 - 8 miles in the direction of the current for the distance represented in the graph by D1+D2.

Combining this value with those of the ZHP to define a rectangular area, we obtain a base Search Zone (ZB) of 6x13 miles, within which the sinking site originally cited in the reports is positioned as shown in the graph.

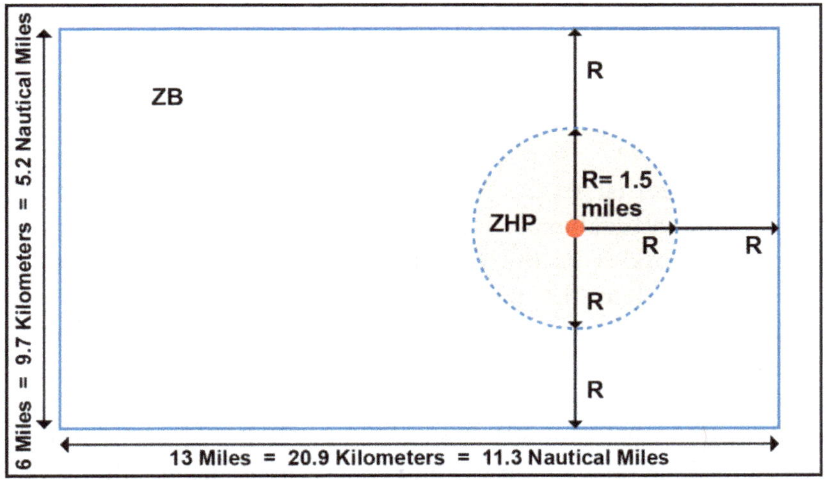

Search Zone (ZB) containing the sinking site cited in the reports and the Probable Sinking Zone (ZHP) generated from this point.

7.5- Priority criteria to follow.

The adoption of a scheme that contains the least favorable sinking scenario is essential, and in this sense, to the extent that the ZB widens, naturally the possibility of containing within it the resting place of the wreck becomes greater. Likewise, managing the exploration of the ZB in an integrated manner is ideal.

However, optimizing the use of exploration resources (time, with all its economic and even meteorological implications) is also key, so that prior establishment of certain priority criteria regarding ZB exploration is equally important.

For this, the ZB is divided into four blocks.

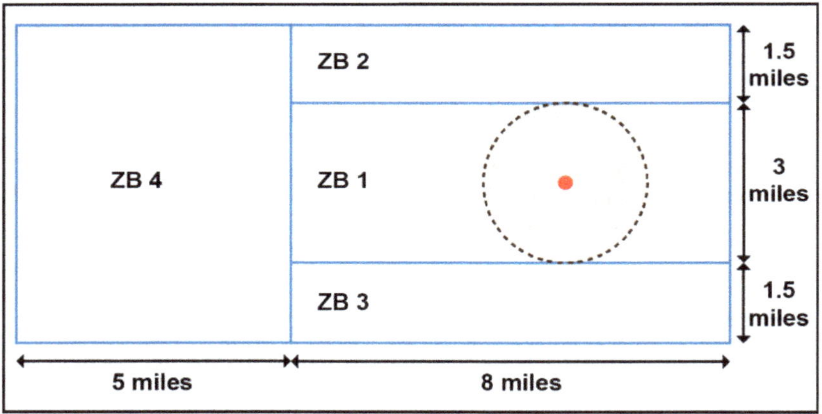

Search Zone segments.

Based on the fact that, of the analyzed scenarios, the most historically accepted is the internal explosion with a relatively abrupt sinking, we give the highest priority to the block identified as ZB 1, which contains the position cited in the reports and also covers the entire area immediately to it, where one might expect the body of the submarine could have fallen under that scenario.

Adjacent zones, ZB 2 and ZB 3, are assigned the following degree of priority, and their exploration would proceed immediately after ZB 1 has been covered in case the wreck has not been located within it.

Lastly, ZB 4 encompasses a more remote area, typical of a notably distant fall like the one described in Scenario 2. Its exploration makes sense, and it would be undertaken, in case the wreck had not been located in the three previous zones.

7.6- Search planning using Side Scan Sonar.

The appropriate technology for the exploration of the surface of the seabed is the Side Scan Sonar. The characteristics of operation of this device (the horizontal range of the lateral acoustic beams and the width of the central dead zone) determine the search strategy, very particularly what refers to the planning and spacing of the routes to follow during the exploration, to effectively cover, without "holes" the planned area.

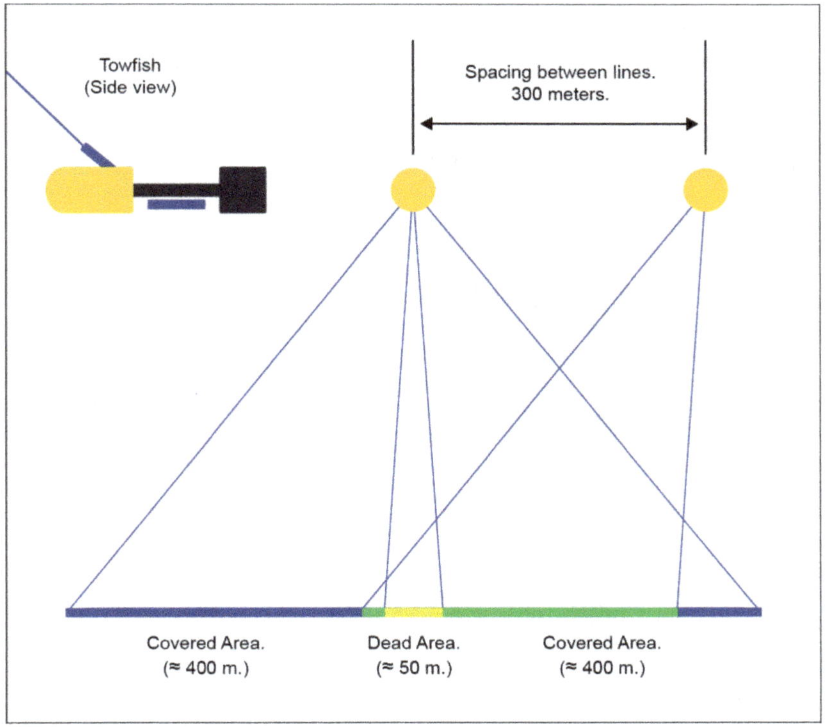

Each of the defined Search Zones should be "scanned" with the Side Scan Sonar. For this, the usual practice consists of longitudinally subdividing the surface of interest by means of imaginary lines that will serve as a route for the ship and the towfish.

Since the dimensions of the target object of the search exceeds several tens of meters (at least in one axis), and it is also metallic, it is feasible to perform a "thick" search, at a frequency of 100KHz. This allows detecting -although without great details- objects with the characteristics that are sought, and makes it feasible a wide scanning range, of approximately 400 meters on each side, which significantly reduces the number of lines necessary to cover the area.

Once the area is covered, a more detailed sweep - at a frequency of 400 KHz - can be carried out on the sites or specific lines that contain elements of interest.

With a spacing of 300 meters between lines (to avoid dead zones in the final result), we obtain for each Search Zone, the following totals for the "coarse search" stage:

Search Zone	**Number of Lines**	**Time per Line. (@2.5 knots)**	**Total time in the ZB.**	**Total scan length.**
1	16 (4828m/300m)	5.2 hours (3.2 h + 2h)	83 hours (1 week)	206 km (12874.75m x 16)
2	8 (2414m/300m)	5.2 hours (3.2 h + 2h)	42 hours (4 days)	103 km
3	8 (2414m/300m)	5.2 hours (3.2 h + 2h)	42 hours (4 days)	103 km
4	32 (9656m/300m)	3.5 hours (2 h + 1.5h)	112 hours (11 days)	257.5 km

- 8 -
DISCUSSION

Through this Research Report, we have exposed the results of the historical study related to the sinking of U-176, which gave us various indications and variables that have been taken into account later to establish an adequate procedure for search and location of the wreck, the main objective of this Research. Through the study carried out, such as the analysis of the incidence of the factors that could influence the trajectory of descent of the submarine in its "dead" displacement until reach its final resting area, , it has been possible to establish several fully justified search areas, through arguments resulting from a compatible technical analysis that have allowed establish a logical exploration "framework" and with the maximum of possible precision, since in no way could its final location be established with metric accuracy.

U-176 Project Report

- 9 -
CONCLUSIONS. (ANNEXES).

We consider that with this Report a response is given to the problems formulated in the Research Project, taking into account the management of the available location data, the analysis of the currents and the foreseeable hydrodynamic implications, which once submitted to study and analysis, provided sufficient basic elements to develop a logical criterion to assess and dimension the Search Zones (ZB), which also allowed to establish a priority in the "action scenarios" for the execution of the search and location process. From now on, only the practical execution of the search, for which it will be necessary the implementation of logistics and technical means, vessel suitable for such work, side scan sonar and ROV (Remoted Operated Vehicle) for exploration, specific lighting equipment and cameras for filming that we suggest.

With all these technical elements within reach, you can proceed to the search, location and filming "in situ" of the wreck that is the object of this study and for this it will be necessary the collaboration of Institutions, Universities, etc., who contribute materially or financially to the success of this endeavor; however, experiences in similar exploration works suggest that the final result allows recover part, if not all, of the financial volume of its realization and even overcome it, and all this, apart from the enormous and important benefits that your study can bring from the point of view Historical - Scientific.

ANNEX I

Technical and aesthetic lighting problems for exploration of the U-176.

Introduction:

The final result of all the exploration work will be visual (photo, video). In this sense, two technical aspects will be vital for project success:

-Lightning.

-Cameras.

Lighting is the first issue to plan, from its technical and aesthetic aspects, according to the objectives of the project and the problem posed by the dimensions of the wreck of the submarine.

The availability of natural light in the work environment, at an estimated depth of 850 meters, will be absolutely zero. Therefore, the equipment must supply artificial lighting, and this requires, on the one hand, energy availability in the remote end under the sea, while on the other, the implementation of a lighting strategy that allows overcoming natural obstacles (attenuation and mirror effect) offered by the marine environment, particularly when operating near the bottom, while promoting the creation of a solid visual product, bearer of integrated information and with aesthetic value.

The human brain, as the final recipient of the images resulting from the exploration, is naturally pre-configured for a certain "visual format" in terms of the information that is provided through the image. Visually capturing the whole that is the object of interest, or at least a significant part of it, is vital for that easy and pleasant mental conformation of an integrated image to take place. Providing a “sequence” of fragmented and punctual of small parts of that same set, would have a very questionable value in every sense.

The problem itself:

Basically, the visual exploration tool of a wreck is constituted by the ROV, which has its own lighting system and cameras with which to illuminate and visually perceive the immediate environment around it.

This scheme is satisfactory and sufficient for specific work, that is, when the set of everything we are interested in capturing it is visually comparable in dimensions with the vehicle and is located near it. Thus, the entire set of interest can be captured in a single image, which is illuminated by the system on board the ROV, with satisfactory results.

However, when trying to obtain a visual perspective of a body whose dimensions are many times larger than those of the ROV itself, such as the wreck of the U-176, the vehicle's own lighting capacity is not enough, and it won't be enough to solve this inconvenience —as might be thought a priori— with simply increasing the lighting power.

Technical and aesthetic reasons:

When a certain amount of light is emitted in a certain direction under the sea, it is important to note that the volume of water into which it will spread is not perfectly transparent: it contains millions of microparticles suspended within the liquid volume that will absorb and reflect small amounts of light (energy), with which, as we move away from the emitting focus, the amount of "effective" available light will undergo severe attenuation.

In practical terms, illuminating a scene under the sea that is a certain number of meters away from the emitting source will require much more "luminous energy" than if we were, say, on land, in clean air conditions.

The solution to this problem is not just a matter of a mere increase in power, as stated before, for two reasons:

Increasing the power of the emitting focus causes the reflection of light caused by the particles suspended in the volume of water to be even greater. These tiny mirrors, when the lighting power is increased beyond a certain level, depending on the surrounding conditions, they literally dazzle the camera, resulting in an image of very questionable quality and of very little value in any way, even for the ROV's own navigation.

Increase the power of the emitter focus in the ROV, even in the unlikely event that the previous problem did not exist, would create very poor-quality lighting from an aesthetic point of view: would cast strong shadows; would constitute a lighting "without fillings", with very little documentary merit.

Distributed lighting scheme:

Managing at least two complementary light sources constitutes an obvious and minimally elementary alternative when we consider this same problem of shadows and light fill from the perspective of a photo or video studio. The exact same visual rules apply to our case, but implementing this at 850 meters under the sea involves somewhat more ingenious and daring procedures.

The proposed solution to implement this scheme takes advantage of the ROV support structure, which is formed not only by the vehicle itself, but also by its cable management system (like a kind of garage), technically known as TMS, or Tether Management System. The TMS is the intermediate link between the vehicle (the ROV) and all surface infrastructure. In operating conditions, the TMS hangs from the ship by means of the umbilical cable, it being usual to leave it about ten meters, maybe fifteen meters, above the bottom.

This hanging structure is very attractive both as a physical support (whose height from the bottom -or from the body of the wreck- can be handled from the surface without any problem) and as an energy support for a complementary light source, especially if we are talking about a Work Class ROV.

This solution, it must be said, is not a new idea: it has already been used in previous explorations in deep waters where -as in the one in question- the film and photographic documentation has played an important role.

Technical feasibility of this solution:

Since in Work Class ROVs the electrical power transmission capacity of the umbilical cables used is usually significant, and furthermore, since the effective electrical consumption of the TMS in idle conditions (once the ROV has undocked and is doing some activity near the bottom) decreases notably, it is feasible to manage an additional electrical load for lighting, which comes into operation once the vehicle is uncoupled.

The power values (in KVA) available will naturally depend on the specific characteristics of the system used. This will require an analysis with the manufacturer's data at hand, or even a TMS adaptation work directly with them (something very common in the industry) to support this additional function.

Operational implications:

The handling of this complementary light source will not only consist of controlling its intensity, but also of its displacement – to give an example – along the wreck to the extent that the vehicle also moves longitudinally in its exploration route.

This last case -the displacement of the light source- requires a close coordination between the ROV control post and the bridge of the ship, which will move the position of the vessel in the indicated direction in a controlled manner (dynamic positioning of the vessel) at a speed similar to what the ROV is having at the bottom.

ANNEX II

Technical requirements for the exploration, with Side Scan Sonar, of the search area determined as probable for the resting place of the wreck of U-176:

Introduction:

Determining the geographical coordinates of the wreck's resting place, at the bottom level, constitutes the first indispensable step towards the final objective of the project, which will be its visual exploration and film documentation.

With this vital information at hand –basically made up of two simple numbers-, a ship equipped with one or two ROVs, equipped with the appropriate lighting and filming resources, it will fix its location on the surface by means of dynamic positioning in the already known coordinates, and it will carry out the exploration and filming work in the background without much difficulty.

However, the process through which these coordinates are obtained is not something exactly simple, expeditious, or exempt from uncertainties and risks: technologically, it is necessary to gain the ability to "see" the bottom surface in the entire area of search selected as probable for the resting place of the wreck, and also, "distinguish" the object of interest on it in order to establish its location.

All this means, broadly speaking:

- The availability -technological and operational- of a side-scan sonar with the capacity and conditions to operate at least at 1,200 meters (the estimated depth at the wreck's resting place is 850 meters); with availability of 4,000 – 4,500 meters of cable; with Dual Frequency capacity - 100-400 kHz - to be able to carry out coarse or detailed scans, as required; with integrated traction system (electro-hydraulic winch) of appropriate capacity for the dynamic handling of this load and automatic level-winder system; electro-hydraulic launch and recovery system (LARS); information monitoring and recording software – generally included as part of the sonar system itself; compatible software for mosaic generation.

- Vessel with dynamic positioning and ability to accurately follow trajectories previously defined in the navigation system at speeds (generally slow) previously defined as well; energy capacity available to handle the loads imposed by the sonar equipment, traction winch and LARS system; equipped with a submarine positioning system (USBL, or Ultra Short Base Line system), to determine in real time the absolute position of the sonar TowFish at the underwater end and integrate it with the monitoring and recording software.

Side Scan Sonar.

The key technology for the search stage for the wreck's resting place is the Side Scan Sonar, a tool that, by acoustic means, sequentially forms an image of the surface of the seabed along a path.

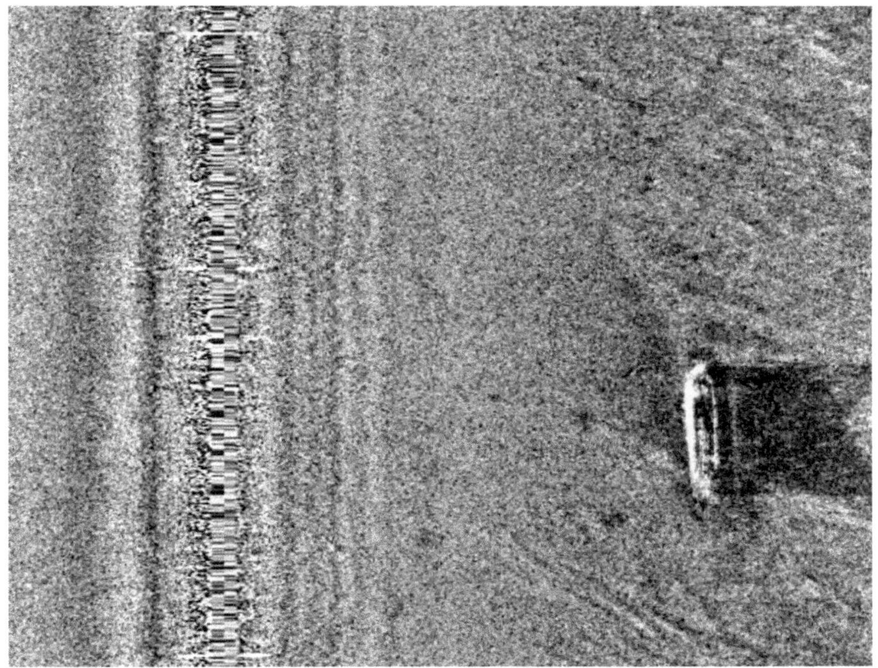

Typical image obtained with a side scan sonar.
On the right, the image of a shipwreck is recognizable.

There are different renowned manufacturers in this field, with more or less similar general characteristics in principle. In a severe and hostile environment such as the marine environment, however, the experience of years is what proves or not the real value of a specific technology.

By way of illustration, and since it is a system with which, in particular, previous work experience has been had in deep waters (with this technology the USS Maine was located off Havana in the year 2000, more than a thousand meters deep), in addition to coming from a top-tier manufacturer (Kongsberg Geoacoustics), the following are the "desirable" features of the Side Scan Sonar system, based on the Deep Tow 2000 platform.

DeepTow 2000 , Kongsberg Geoacoustics.

Platform robustness.

Essential for the work to be done. The 136SS platform (on which the Deep Tow 2000 is built) is definitely robust, of adequate mass to work at intended depths (it is designed to reach 2,000 meters as nominal depth, maximum up to 3,500 meters) and above all it is stable: it does not present significant mechanical vibrations when it is operated, which is a very appreciated quality because it does not introduce noise (remember that the principle of operation of the sonar is vibratory: acoustic).

The appearance of the mass is significant from a practical point of view at the depths at which it is intended to work. A light Tow Fish, as there are many, are more for shallow waters (in most cases they can be carried by one person, and they are operated from a yacht). As they are intended to be used in deep waters, to reach the operating depth, their low weight makes it necessary to "pull out" an excessive amount of cable, which can even constitute an operating hazard because when it ends up being heavier it can touch the bottom, getting entangled with some natural or artificial obstacle, etc.

This particular was discussed by the author with specialists from Kongsberg Geoacoustics, reaching a consensus on both sides that, moreover, supports the experience.

Required amount of cable.

The rule of thumb for determining the recommended amount of cable to operate at a given depth is approximately 4.5*D, where D is the depth. With this, for a thousand meters (the depth of the wreck is estimated at 850 meters, but conservatively for the calculation we use 1000 meters) we are talking about 4,500 meters of cable.

This cable covers a double function: mechanical and electrical. In addition to mechanically pulling the vehicle, through it electrical energy is supplied to the TowFish electronics and control information and data are exchanged between both ends, surface and submarine.

Dual Frequency capability.

The ability to operate at two different frequencies (114 kHz – 410 kHz in the case of the DeepTow 2000) is a highly desirable feature for optimizing operation, in particular when what is sought to find is an object with the dimensions of the wreck of the U-176 and, moreover, of entirely metallic construction.

In the case of the U-176, both characteristics of the wreck are very favorable when Dual Frequency is available, since it allows optimization of the search in terms of time and economic resources.

With the lower frequency (longer wavelength) extensions of up to 400 meters on each side of the sonar path can be covered, but without great detail. The latter means that the sonar will not be able to distinguish an object, say, maybe 4 or 5 meters long half buried in the bottom and made of wood, but it will surely perceive a body over 50 meters long, especially a metallic one, since it will cause an echo intense enough to be recorded by the equipment's sensors. Though blurry in terms of lack of detail, the detection of a body with these characteristics and a figure more or less similar to the one that could be expected from the wreck of the submarine will be unequivocal, will draw attention and justify a new sweep on that line now with more detail, or what is the same to say, using a higher frequency.

With the higher frequency (shorter wavelength) the extension to the sides that the sonar is capable of covering is not so great, but knowing in advance where the object that caught the attention is, the line of travel can be re-planned without difficulty for one of the two sonar beams to literally "pass over" him. The image that results from this sweep, without a doubt, will tell if it is the object sought or not.

Electro-hydraulic winch.

The operation of the Side Scan Sonar, from the mechanical point of view, is governed through a winch located in the stern area of the ship. The practical experience of operating this equipment -and our staff in particular- attest that this is a component of the system that is often underestimated when allocating resources to a project, perhaps because it is not the most spectacular part since technological point of view, which is a very serious mistake that can lead directly to the loss of the sonar, with the consequent economic and moral impact.
The operation of the Side Scan Sonar, from the mechanical point of view, is governed through a winch located in the stern area of the ship. The practical experience of operating these machines -and ours in particular- attest that this is a component of the system that is very often underestimated when allocating resources to a project, perhaps because it is not the most spectacular part from a technological point of view, which is a very serious mistake that can lead directly to the loss of the sonar, with the consequent economic and moral.

Unfortunately, a proper winch can cost even more than the Side Scan Sonar itself.

The use of an electrohydraulic winch designed for dragging platforms under the sea is recommended (such is the case of a tow fish); with an appropriate dynamic response to react unambiguously to emergencies and unforeseen events that are a natural part of the exploration process with side scan sonar; with the necessary automatic functions for cable winding management (automatic level winder).

After discussing this point with the technical staff of Kongsberg Geoacoustics, and based on the operating experience accumulated with its DeepTow 2000 system by different clients around the world for nearly fifteen years, the acceptability characteristics of the winch were defined as follows:

- ***Type:*** Electro-hydraulic.
- ***Motor:*** 37.5 kW, 3 Phase, 480 V, 60 Hz.
- ***Drum capacity:*** 4,500 m of steel armored coaxial cable, 11.4 mm drag.
- ***Linear speed at Drum level:*** 0-60 m/min.
- ***Traction capacity at Drum level:*** 2.7 Tons.
- ***Brake system:*** Operated from joystick control, and independent manual brake.
- ***Level Wind:*** Hydro-active type, automatic, with bidirectional cable angle sensor, both manual and automatic.
- ***Construction:*** A-36 steel with stainless steel accessories.

There are several options in the market, standing out among the manufacturers of marine winches, the MacArtney and Dynacon companies.

Winch with characteristics approximately similar to those described, in this case from the MacArtney company.

The use of an inappropriate winch, based on improvisation criteria as a way to "optimize economic resources", in addition to a great ignorance of the rigors of this activity, can lead directly to the loss of equipment and/or severe damage to the physical integrity of the personnel involved in its operation.

Launch and Recovery Systems (LARS).

Safely moving the Tow Fish from the deck to the water (both for the equipment and for the personnel involved in the operation), and vice versa, is not a trivial operation by any means since we are talking about a component whose mass is around of 200Kg and that, moreover, is in a pendulum, hanging from a cable at the mercy of the constant rocking of the boat. In addition, supporting the mechanical loads implied by its traction under the sea is not something trivial either.

Both functions are carried out by the Launch And Recovery System (LARS).

Most vessels involved in scientific research operations, or industrial inspection and construction work, have some type of LARS. It is therefore necessary to consider this point when selecting a vessel.

Small Launch and Retrieve System, used in the illustrated case to operate a small ROV, but generally similar to that used for a Tow Fish.

Manually managing the launch or recovery operation, even in calm sea conditions, can be a very risky maneuver for personnel.

The ship.

The vessel on which the side-scan sonar exploration work will be carried out may or may not be the same on which the ROV exploration and filming will subsequently be carried out.

In any case, it must have at least two important qualities:

Dynamic positioning.

It is the ability of a ship to maintain itself automatically, with an error of very few meters, in a specific geographical position, all of this also maintaining the course that has been specified.

Most modern vessels engaged in industrial subsea work are originally equipped, by design, with a dynamic positioning system. This system is made up of a group of propellers (in addition to those of the basic propulsion system) whose orientation and power is regulated by an automatic control platform that, based on the coordinates obtained via GPS, maintain the ship in a certain position and course without human intervention.

Since side-scan sonar exploration requires the vessel to travel at a given speed, without deviation, along a previously designed set of parallel line traces loaded into the navigation system, this in order to unequivocally cover the entire area of planned search, the dynamic positioning system is essential.

In the case of exploration with ROV, the reasoning is similar: the position of the vessel must be strictly fixed on the surface so as not to drag the equipment that operates on the bottom. Or, when required, it must move at a controlled speed, in a specified direction, to reproduce on the surface the route that the ROV will be making on the bottom.

Underwater acoustic positioning: Ultra-Short Baseline System.

The ship's surface coordinates are easily obtainable through GPS. Unfortunately, things are more difficult underwater, and it is essential, on the other hand, to know the coordinates of the equipment that is being operated: Tow Fish or ROV.

The way this is achieved is by determining the relative position of the underwater vehicle relative to the ship. Thus, knowing the global position of the ship (coordinates provided by the GPS) and knowing the spatial position of the vehicle with respect to the ship, the absolute global position of the vehicle can be calculated.

The technology that acts as GPS under the sea is known as the Ultra Short Base Line system, and it is, in essence, a spatial acoustic measurement system.

Its operation is simple in principle: an antenna of four spaced hydrophones X, located under the hull of the ship, periodically emits an acoustic signal that, when perceived by a transponder unit mounted on the underwater vehicle (a beacon), will generate for this also an acoustic response. The antenna and USBL system on board will listen to it, and from the elapsed time, calculate how far away the responding beacon is, and in what direction, which, combined as said with the GPS information for the ship, will allow to mathematically construct the absolute position of the vehicle under the sea.

Inside the red circle, head of the beacon installed on the Tow Fish, to obtain its position through the USBL system of the ship. The arrow points to the cylinder that houses the beacon electronics.

Not all boats are equipped with these types of systems. Rather, they include those dedicated to scientific missions or industrial work under the sea. This, naturally, will be part of the selection criteria for the boat to finally be used.

- 10 -
SOURCES CONSULTED:

Bibliography.

-**Churchill, S. Wiston; D. Rooselvelt, Franklin y F.Kimball, Warren;** "Churchill & Rooselvelt: the complete correspondence". Princeton, N.J.; Princeton University Press. 1984.

-**Elliot Morrison, Samuel,** "The Two-Ocean War: A Short History of the United States Navy in the Second World War", Naval Institute Press 2007.

-**Gaylord T.M. Kelshall,** "The U-boat war in the Caribbean", Naval Institute Press, USA, 1994.

-**Gómez Álvarez, Maximino;** "U-boats del III Reich en Cuba", Entrelineas Editores, Madrid, 2009.

-**Gómez Álvarez, Maximino;** "El Incidente 3208: hundimiento del U-176", (inédito).

-**Niestle, Axel,** "German U-boats Losses During World War II: Details of Destruction" . United States Naval Inst. 1998.

-**Norberto Collado Abreu,** "Collado: Timonel del Granma", Casa Editorial Verde Olivo; La Habana. 2006.

-**Rohwer, Jürgen and Hümmelchen, Gerhard,** "Chronology of the War at Sea 1939-1945". United States Naval Inst. 1992.

-**Thomas, Hugh,** "Cuba, la lucha por la libertad", Edi. Random House, USA, 2004.

-**Wyn, Kenneth,** "U-boats Operations of the Second World War", volume I, Cahrtham Publisher 1997.

Press.

-**Revista Bohemia:** Lara Cabañas, Ernesto M., "Héroes, marinos cubanos", La Habana, mayo 15 2003.
-**Periódico Trabajadores:** Placer Cervera, Gustavo "Hundimiento del submarino alemán U-176", La Habana, mayo 15 2013.

Archives (Primary Sources).

-Bundesarchiv, Militärarchiv,
Freiburg Im Breisgau. Germany.
-Personal Collection Of Oswald Kulik,
Hamburg, Germany.
-Personal Collection Of Richard Zeni,
San Antonio, California. United States.
-Deparment Of Navy, Naval Historical Center,
Washington D.C. United States.
-Deutsches Schifffahrtsmuseum ,
Bremerhaven, Hamburg. Germany.
-National Archives And Records Administration (Nara).
Records Relating To U-Boat Warfare, 1939-1945.
Adelphy Road, College Park; Md. United States.
-U-Boot-Archiv,
Cuxhaven-Altembruch, Germany.

Internet.

-Histamar, http://www.histarmar.com.ar/InfHistorica/CaribeyWW2.htm
-National Geophysical Data Center, mapgdc.nooa.gov
-Splinter Fleet (http://www.splinterfleet.org)
-Uboot.net. The uboat War 1939-1945
-Uboatarchiv.net
-Uboatases.com
-U Historia. U-176
-Ubootwaffw.net (http://www.ubootwaffe.net/)
-Uboats in Bahamas ericwiberg.com/Bahamas

Interviews.

- Eick, Alfred	Former officer of U-176 and Commander of U-510.
- Bredow, Horst	Director Boot Archiv (former U-288 crewman).
- Kulik, Oswald	Former U-625 and U-965 crew member (Germany).
- Merderd, Danward	Former Aviation Officer R.F.A (Germany).
- Zeni, Richard	US Navy, VS-62 Squadron. (USA)

ABOUT THE AUTHORS

Maximino Gomez Alvarez (28 November 1952 – 25 October 2022). BA in History from the University of Havana; Museologist; post-graduate degrees in Naval History, Research Methodology, Ethnology and Archiveology. He received several awards and mentions for his research, including: "V Meeting of Researchers of Cultural Heritage", Cuba (two mentions in the category of History); "VIII Symposium of Culture of the City", Cuba, (1st Prize in History). He participated in various international events, "X Conference of Archive Directors of Eastern Countries", "II International Conference on Conservation of Heritage and Historic Centers" and "Message to the World" among others. He has given talks and conferences. He also collaborated with the Cuban magazine of Social Sciences.

* * * * * * *

Alexander Mirabal Reyes. Engineer, "Gold Diploma", Bachelor of Telecommunications at the University of Havana, Cuba. Specialist, among others, in the integration of fiber optic connection systems for operation with mini-submarines, as well as in the design and implementation of personalized signal distribution systems for submersible operations and in Deep Water Positioning Systems. He worked as a ROV (Remote Operated Vehicle) Pilot; in the Scientific Research Ship "Ulises", contracted by the Canadian company Advanced Digital Communications, exploring the northern zone of the western coast of Cuba (in a depth range of 500 to 1,500 meters) in the identification of shipwrecks to later be explored and filmed by ROV; As a result of this work, dozens of wrecks were explored and filmed off the coast of Havana, the most relevant being the remains of the battleship "USS Maine", a US warship that suffered an explosion that caused its sinking in the port of Havana in 1898, an event that triggered the Spanish-American War and that was refloated in 1912 and then sunk again in the open sea.

In this search, location and filming operation at a depth of 1,500 meters, Engineer Alexander Mirabal had the privilege of being in charge of it, as Technical Specialist and ROV Pilot. This event was widely reviewed by some US newspapers and other media, especially in Florida, where the USF (University of South Florida) followed this work with interest.

He also actively participated in the discovery and filming of the megalithic structures announced by some international media as a "sunken city" in the western end of the Island of Cuba (Cabo San Antonio). His works are collected in documentaries such as "Buscar al Maine" by Public Broadcasting Corporation and La Nueva "Aventura del Ulises", made for the Cuban TV.

Alexander Mirabal currently continues to work at the prestigious Oceaneering International Company as a Specialist Technician and ROV Pilot. He is a member of the AIDHNC History Section.

* * * * * * *

Osvaldo L Cangas. (16 October 1992)
BA in History, MA in Sociology; Post-graduate Degrees in Museology, Museography, and Museums Studies, Expert in Cultural Heritage Conservation, World War I and World War II Studies, Military History, Research Methodology.

Has participated in several international courses and seminaries carried out in different countries such as Argentina, Bolivia, Costa Rica, Spain, the United Kingdom, etc.

Founder and Director of the U-176 Museum-Institute for War Studies Inc, in Miami, FL. He is also current member of several national and international organizations such as the ICOM "International Council of Museums", Small Museum Association, American Historical Association and the American Alliance of Museums.

The realization of this translation has been possible thanks to the collaboration and joint work of our organizations. An arduous task whose main objective is the disclosure and preservation of naval-military history, and in this specific case, to make possible the disclosure of the events that occurred on May 15, 1943, the day the SubChaser CS-13 of the Cuban Navy, in military action, confronted and sank the Nazi U-Boat U-176.

In this textual material, the possible location of this wreck is detailed, as well as the possible ways to reach it for documentary filming, and the recommendations of experts in the field.

Asociación para la Investigación y
Difusión de la Historia Naval de Cuba.
&
U-176 Museum-Institute for War Studies Inc.

For reproduction permits and for purchase of this book in quantities for promotional or premium use, discounts and terms,
please contact us at social@u-176.com – www.u-176.com
Mailing Address: 11241 SW 157th Street. Miami, FL. 33157.

Miami, Florida.
USA

Asociación para la Investigación y Difusión de la Historia Naval de Cuba.

&

U-176 Museum-Institute for War Studies Inc.

Our organizations are constantly investigating and publishing military historical material, we have several titles available for distribution, if your library or anybody you know would like to obtain copies of our books for adding to a catalogue then please contact us at librarydept@u-176.com **or at** social@u-176.com – www.u-176.com

Mailing Address: 11241 SW 157th Street. Miami, FL. 33157.

Your help spreading the word about our organizations is much appreciated!

www.ingramcontent.com/pod-product-compliance
Lightning Source LLC
LaVergne TN
LVHW010358160826
845677LV00005BA/1311

* 9 7 9 8 3 4 8 1 1 7 7 0 2 *